ABCEDAR

An Alphabet of Trees

by George Ella Lyon
designed and illustrated by Tom Parker

Orchard Books / New York
a division of Franklin Watts, Inc.

A B C D E F G H I J K L M

Orchard Books, 387 Park Avenue South, New York, New York 10016
Orchard Books Great Britain, 10 Golden Square, London W1R 3AF England
Orchard Books Australia, 14 Mars Road, Lane Cove, New South Wales, 2066
Orchard Books Canada, 20 Torbay Road, Markham, Ontario 23P 1G6

Orchard Books is a division of Franklin Watts, Inc.

Manufactured in the United States of America.
The text of this book is set in Futura Extra Bold.
The illustrations are India ink with photo-mechanically applied colors.

10 9 8 7 6 5 4 3 2 1

Library of Congress Cataloging-in-Publication Data
Lyon, George Ella, 1949-
A B Cedar: an alphabet of trees / by George Ella Lyon;
designed and illustrated by Tom Parker.
Summary: An alphabet book introducing the leaves from a variety of trees.
ISBN 0-531-05795-X.   ISBN 0-531-08395-0 (lib. bdg.)
1. Trees—Identification—Juvenile literature. 2. Leaves—Identification—
Juvenile literature. 3. English language—Alphabet—Juvenile literature. [1.
Trees—Identification. 2. Leaves—Identification. 3. Alphabet.]
I. Parker, Tom, ill. II. Title.

QK477.2.I4L96 1989   582.16—dc19   [E]
88-22797   CIP   AC

NOPQRSTUVWXYZ

A B C D E F G H I J K L M

NOPQRSTUVWXYZ

A stand of trees

A B █ █ E F G H I J K L

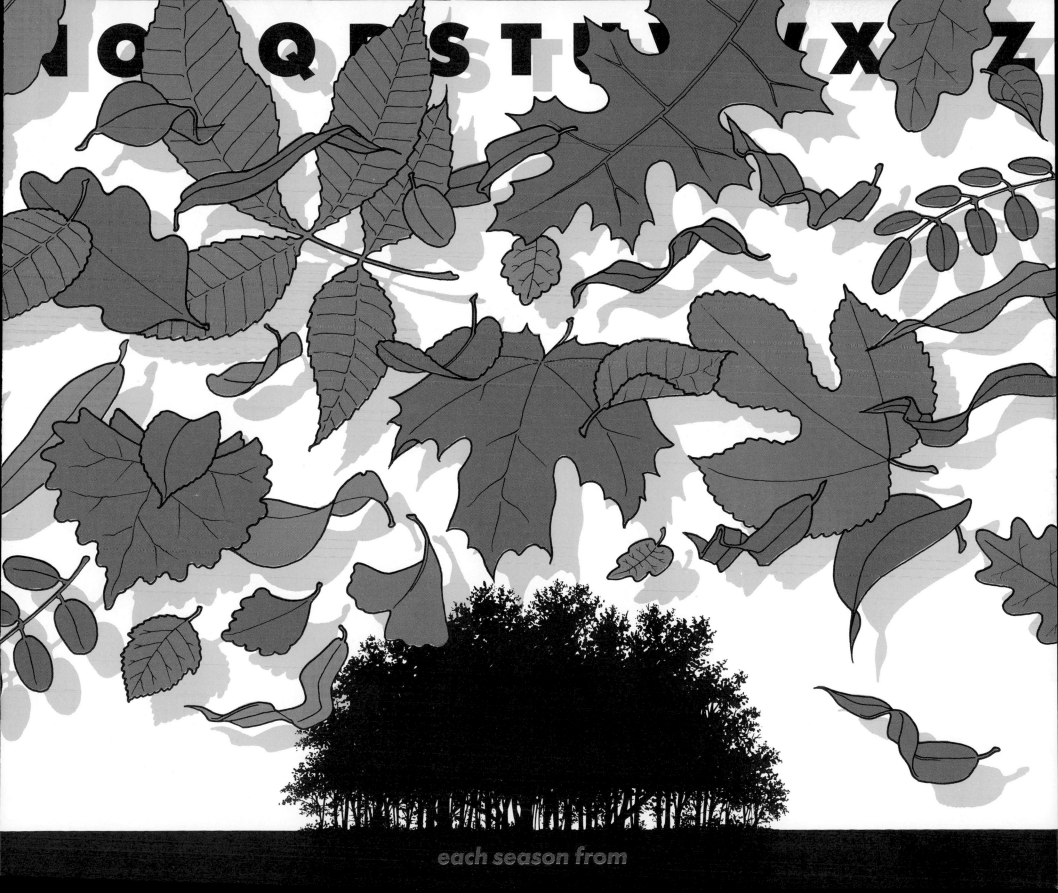

each season from

ABCDEFGH KLM

ASPEN

BUTTERNUT

CEDAR

F I R

GINKGO

HICKORY   IRONWOOD

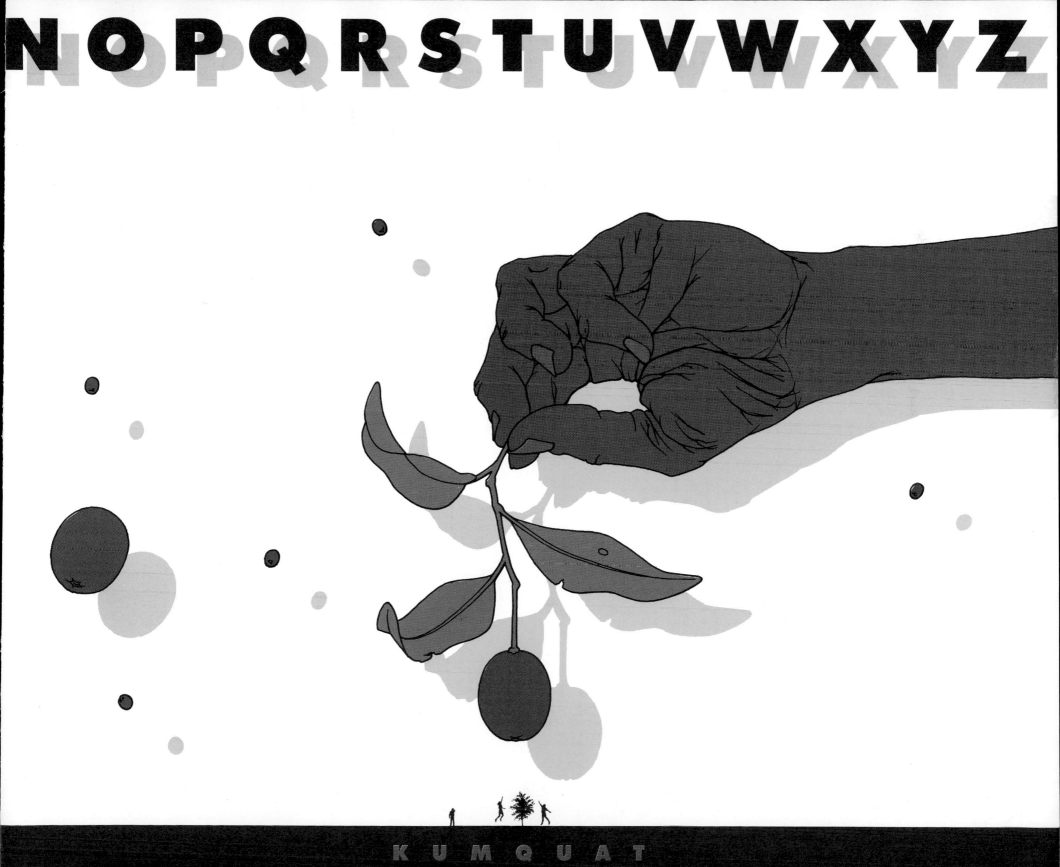

NOPQRSTUVWXYZ

KUMQUAT

ABCDEFGHIJKLM

MAPLE NANNYBERRY

OAK

POPLAR

QUINCE

A B C D E F G H I J K L M

UMBRELLA TREE

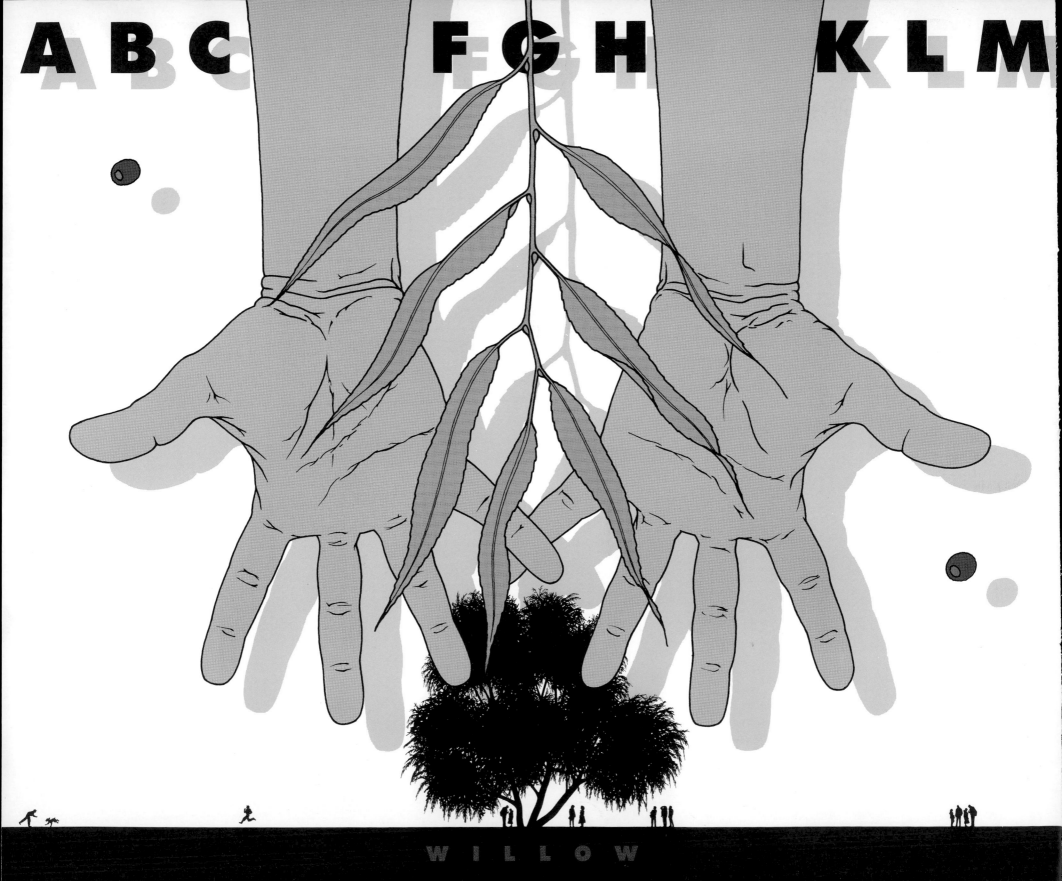

XOLISMA   YEW

ABCDEFGHIJKLM

ZEBRAWOOD

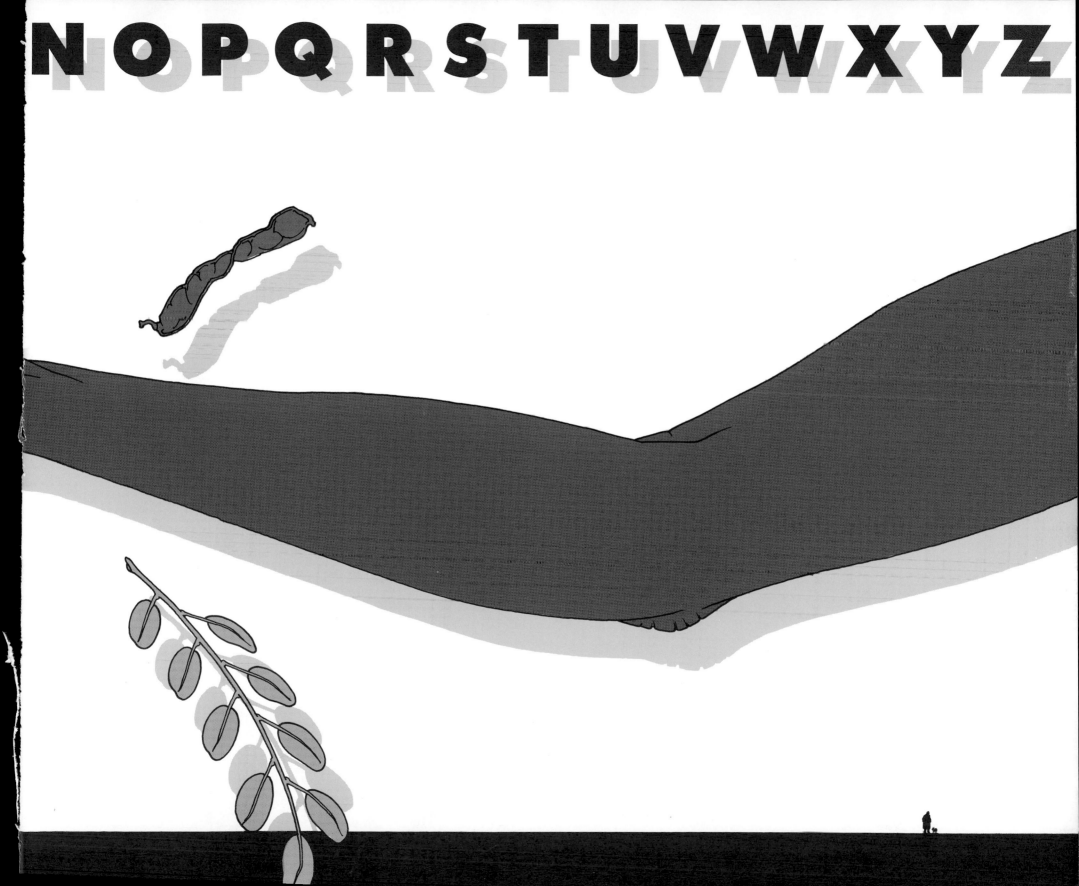

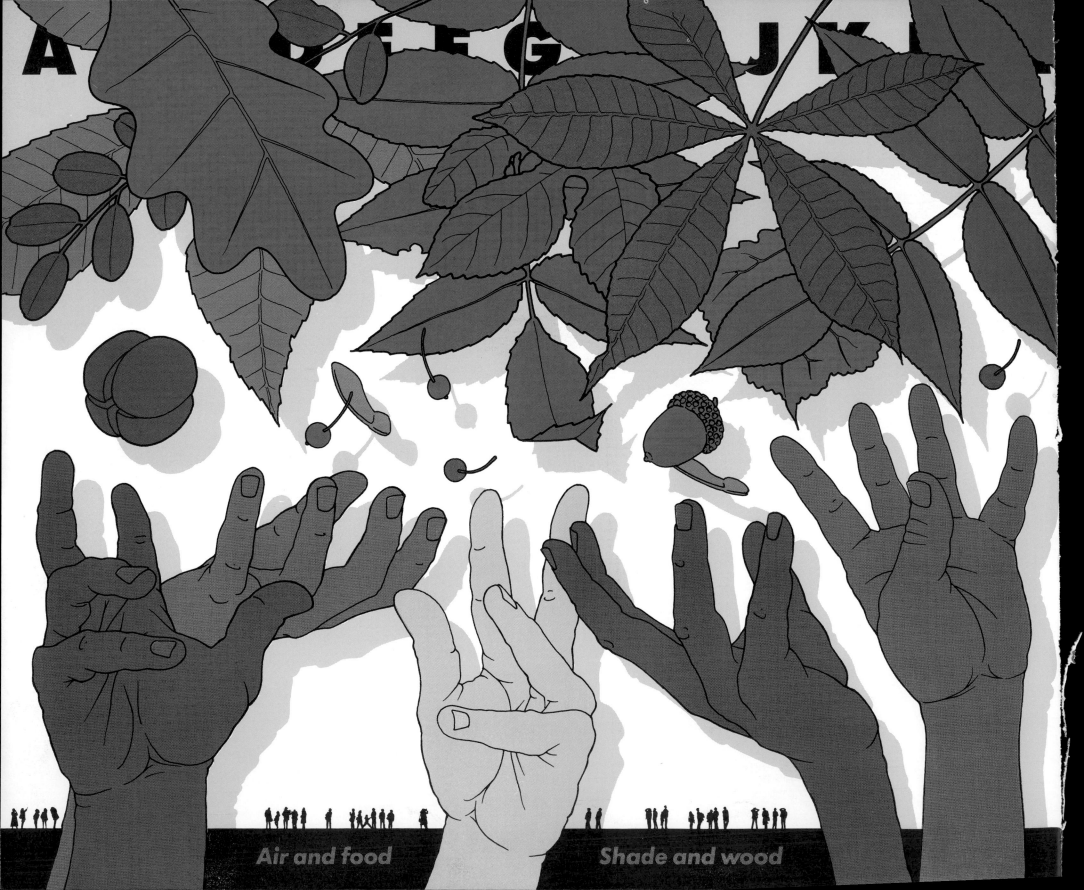

Air and food   Shade and wood

Trees give us

A stair to climb

A place to look

Even this book!